BEAUTIFUL

By the Editors of Sunset Books and Sunset Magazine

LANE MAGAZINE & BOOK COMPANY,

CALIFORNIA

A Sunset Pictorial

Book Editor: Dorothy Krell
Design and Typography: William Gibson

MENLO PARK, CALIFORNIA

CONTENTS

Executive Editor, Sunset Books: David E. Clark

All rights reserved throughout the world. Second Edition. Copyright©1969, 1963 by Lane Magazine & Book Company, Menlo Park, California. No part of this publication may be reproduced by any mechanical, photographic, or electronic-process, or in the form of a phonographic recording, nor may it be stored in a retrieval system, transmitted, or otherwise copied for public or private use without prior written permission from the publisher. Library of Congress No. 63-11739. SBN Title No. 376-05032-2. Lithographed in the U.S.A. Seventh Printing June 1975.

Photographs below (left to right) by:
Richard Dawson, Josef Muench, Richard Dawson,
Martin Litton, John Robinson.

BEAUTIFUL CALIFORNIA

In the richness of its diversity, the grandeur of its scenic attractions, and the excitement of its visual contrasts, California stirs those who know it to hyperbole and extravagant appreciation. If Californians tend to write or talk too much or too exuberantly about their state, bear with them—for they are enraptured by the natural beauty of their golden land.

In a very real sense, this fortunate state compresses within its boundaries the scenic features of an entire continent: seashore, desert, mountain ranges, navigable rivers, waterfalls, landlocked harbors, farming plains, glaciers, perpetual snow, slumbering volcanoes, lakes and inland seas.

Most of the state's scenic diversity derives from the unique arrangement of its mountains, valleys, and rivers; its long shoreline that stretches a distance equivalent to that between Boston, Massachusetts, and Charleston, South Carolina; and the extremes in altitude and climate contained within its borders, ranging from elevations of minus 279 feet to 14,495 feet above sea level, from temperature extremes of a chilly minus 45° to a searing 134°, of rainfall ranging from a trace to 100 inches a year, and of snowfall that is unknown throughout most of the state but has been measured at 70 feet on a Sierra summit.

The contrasts start at the surf line. Along its tortuous twelve hundred miles of alternating beach and bluff, the coast stretches from a sunny, subtropical beachland, washed by temperate ocean currents, to fog-ridden, wave-battered headlands in the north—from palm groves to conifer forests. A coastal shelf runs along beside the sea, squeezed between the mountains of the Coast Range and the ocean. In places, the shelf broadens out into open plains or river valleys where the major cities cluster; elsewhere, it narrows to a shallow ledge above the surf, forcing the scattered settlements to cling to the bluffs and the sides of the river inlets.

Magnificent landlocked bays provide natural harbors for the port cities of San Diego and San Francisco; and where the engineering processes of geologic change have failed to serve man's interests, extensive ports have been dredged to form the harbors of Los Angeles and Long Beach.

A series of mountain chains, rising to the 14,000-foot climax of the Sierra Nevada escarpment, intercepts the Pacific's storms and draws down upon the western slopes the rains that nurture the towering redwoods and the thousands of square miles of forest that blanket a third of the state. In the lower elevations, the forests grow in park-like groves of mixed evergreens and deciduous trees: redwoods, madrones, maples, oaks, cedars, firs, and laurels. In the fall they don a bright tartan of orange, amber, and rust, crossed with the dark green of the conifers, when autumn splashes the foliage. In the higher elevations, dense stands of pine, juniper, and fir sweep solidly over the mountainsides.

Within the mountain system lie the gorges, craggy peaks, and the lakes and rivers that delight the eye with their tranquility or overwhelm the viewer with their austere grandeur: the jagged granite wonderland of the Trinity Alps, the gentle landscape of the Kern Plateau, the bold domes of Yosemite rising above the conifers, or azure-blue Lake Tahoe, encircled by forested mountains.

Nestled between the mountain ranges lie innumerable pastoral valleys, checkerboarded with green squares of row-crops, vineyards, pastures, and orchards irrigated by the natural runoff from the encircling heights or by water piped from the great catchbasin that stretches along the crest of the Sierra Nevada. The vast trough of the Central Valley, largest of the agricultural valleys, covers a flatland 450 miles long and 50 miles wide in the heart of the state. Rich and fertile, the valley's great patchwork quilt of farms and ranches produces a substantial percentage of the nation's truck crops. A dozen rivers flow into the valley from the encompassing mountains, but only one leaves it through a gap in the Coast Range. The streams empty into two major rivers—the Sacramento and the San Joaquin—and these come together in a maze of sloughs, lakes, channels, and marshlands known as "The Delta" before making the solo run to the sea beyond the Golden Gate.

Behind the mountain barrier, the wastes of the Mojave and Colorado deserts fill the southeastern quarter of the state. Denied a proportional share of the rains by the intercepting mountains, the barren hills and plains are either seared free of vegetation or lightly clothed with the picturesque plants that are adapted to the hot, dry conditions. Where water has been piped to the parched soil, the desert is shaded by airy groves of date palms, covered with early crops of melons, lettuce, and cotton, or graced with oasis-like communities and resorts.

Although most of California's visual appeal is in its natural landscape, some of its most spectacular sights are the products of man's handiwork. The challenge of the jumbled landforms themselves has produced the great bridges that span San Francisco Bay, the sweeping highways that snake through the mountain passes, and the white, storied city of San Francisco perched on its forty hills. The viewer is overwhelmed by the astonishing sweep of metropolitan Los Angeles, which turns into a sequined sea at night, and by the interweaving freeways that slice intricate patterns through the limitless city. The visitor long remembers the view of San Diego from Point Loma, the esplanade of Santa Barbara, and the windows of the Berkeley-Oakland hills reflecting the setting sun.

The buildings and mementos of California's romantic past add a nostalgic note to the landscape. The growth of the state has been so rapid and all-encompassing that the evidences of the early ways of life have been all but submerged. The few relics that have survived are doubly treasured for the very fact that they have escaped destruction and for the contrast and perspective they provide in a young land.

South of Sonoma, the principal remainders are those left behind by the Spaniards, who occupied California as remote colonists of the Spanish and Mexican empires up to the time of the American take-over just before the Gold

Rush. The territory belonged to Spain for nearly three centuries, but the Spaniards left it alone for two hundred years and did not attempt to colonize it until the 1770's. In their eighty years' occupancy, they built missions, presidios, and haciendas in the coastal valleys, close to rivers or to the ocean where the supply galleons touched port. Although these structures were built of soluble adobe and many were subsequently abandoned for decades, some have miraculously survived to the present day or have been restored to their original form. These fine old buildings have inspired periodic revivals of interest in Spanish architecture, reflected in a large number of Spanish-style public buildings and homes scattered over the state.

The Spanish idyl was too good to last. More powerful nations than aging Spain had their sights trained on this domain, which was known to be well endowed but poorly defended. Russia established a colony at Bodega, 100 miles north of San Francisco, in 1812, and the Spaniards were too weak to do more than protest. When Mexico revolted against Spain in 1822, California joined the rebel cause and became a province of the Empire of Mexico. Still remote from the seat of authority, the native *Californios* went their own way, enjoying the hospitable life of the ranchos and indulging in occasional bloodless revolutions. Americans began to trickle into the province by sea and by land, attracted by the tales carried east by the crews of the trading vessels that for years had been exchanging manufactured goods for the hides and tallow from the ranchos.

In due time, the inevitable happened. United States military forces seized the territory in 1846 soon after the start of the War with Mexico. The *Californios* put up a brief but spirited resistance and then capitulated. The territory was ceded to the United States by the treaty ending the Mexican war in 1848, and two years later, Congress admitted California to the Union.

The California that became a state in 1850 was quite different from the California that the armed forces had seized four years earlier—for in this brief interval, the Gold Rush had begun, completely changing its character. Tides of Yankees and gold-seekers from all over the world flooded into the sleepy little colony. Population jumped from 15,000 in 1847 to 380,000 in 1860. The center of commercial gravity shifted north from Monterey to San Francisco. The great Central Valley—almost completely ignored by the Spaniards—became overspread with farms and cattle ranches. Towns and cities, roads and rail lines, dams and flumes sprouted suddenly where none had existed before.

The relics of these hectic years are clustered in certain sections of northern California, principally the Sierra foothills, where they decay in gentle dignity. Since most of the early buildings were abandoned after the Gold Rush faded, only a relatively small number remain to enchant the traveler, most of them having succumbed to the destruction of the elements, fire, or the "borrowings" of later settlers. Where buildings were built of stone and iron, they have survived picturesquely to the present day. Unfortunately for antiquarians, the key city of the Gold Rush days, San Francisco, lost the relics of its tempestuous past in a series of conflagrations, climaxed by the holocaust of 1906.

The Gold Rush launched the state on a dizzying course of spiraling growth that has continued with ups and downs ever since. The completion of the transcontinental railroad in 1869 and its extension to southern California a few years later drew thousands of settlers to "the perfect paradise, the land of perpetual spring." Industries followed—oil, motion pictures, manufacturing, airplanes—and people poured in to work or simply to live in this bountiful state.

The floodtide of visitors and residents has been flowing into California for a century, as people have come to see for themselves if the state is as beautiful as advertised. They have come, have liked what they found, and have settled down to man the industries and enjoy the western way of living. But the tide continues without let-up, and in time the ceaseless flow may someday submerge the beauties of California as it has nearly obliterated the relics of its past. Most Californians have thus far fought vigorously to protect the natural beauties of their state against the onslaught, and it is to be hoped that this restraint will be as vigilantly continued by those newly arrived and yet to come.

KEY TO CALIFORNIA'S GEOGRAPHICAL HIGHLIGHTS

1. North Coast
2. San Francisco Bay Area
3. Central Coast
4. South Coast
5. Desert
6. Southern Mountains
7. Sierra Nevada
8. Gold Country
9. Central Valley
10. Northern Mountains

THE NORTH COAST

The North Coast is a land of loneliness—of rolling fog and dripping trees, of breakers smashing against rocky bluffs, of dark forests, abandoned lumber towns and logged-off hillsides. But it is also a land of champagne air and sparkling sunshine, a tonic rendezvous for vacationers, a place where rivers run smooth and swift, and venerable little towns with a New England look serve fine chowders, cheese, and wine to the traveler. It is an area that history has touched, as its polyglot place names reveal—Noyo, Point Reyes, Fort Ross, Albion, Valley Ford tell the visitor that Indians, Spaniards, Russians, Englishmen, and Yankees all have had a hand in shaping the destiny of this haunting land.

For its full length, the North Coast is a rugged province where the mountains march straight into the sea and the stubborn cliffs explode the smashing breakers in a spectacle of titanic conflict. Here and there, the coastline opens to an occasional stretch of sandy beach or curves inland to form sheltered coves, beyond the range of the pounding sea. Picturesque fishing villages cling to the sides of the inlets, embracing waterborne forests of masts and spars that rise and fall with the tide when the fleet is in.

Here is the home of the giant redwood, ancient stately trees that soar skyward in softly-lit, cathedral-like groves a few miles inland from the sea. Nearly as old as Western Civilization, the great trees humble the reverent viewer with their antiquity and their majestic proportions.

The works of man add a nostalgic note to the landscape. Most of the ranch houses, barns, and stores were built by an earlier generation with simple materials and from simple plans. Miles of zigzag, split-rail fencing and windbreaks of dark, tangled cypress accompany the leisurely roads. Even man's discards have a melancholy attraction. Abandoned lumber towns, wharves, and mills recall the days when great quantities of lumber were processed and shipped from the once-busy towns along this shore.

Over all this country rolls the intermittent fog, sometimes high and gray and turning everything to monochrome, sometimes scudding over at rooftop, and sometimes clinging close to the ground, where it muffles the roar of the breakers and the rush of the wind through the great trees.

MARTIN LITTON

SEA RANCH

*THE SEA IS QUIET at times in the northernmost corner of California.
Often it is tipped with gold as the last rays of a late-afternoon sun play
upon its surface. In other moments it is a wild sea, and breakers boom as they
crash over jagged rocks. For much of the distance from Crescent City to Eureka,
the Redwood Highway stays close to this rugged, lonely shore, where
picnickers and beachcombers explore sheltered coves and rocky crescents of
wave-washed beach, and fishermen try their luck from shore or boat.*

A SPIDERY BRIDGE here and there connects the two halves of a fishing village that clings to the shores of a river mouth. Tightly packed fleets of small vessels rest on the quiet water. The boats weigh anchor in the misty dawn and chug out to the open sea, returning at nightfall with their catch of salmon and accompanied by clouds of raucous gulls.

BILLOWY BLANKETS OF FOG frequently roll inland from the ocean, first filling the river valleys with a chill mist, then veiling the dark forests, and finally engulfing the mountain crests in a sea of cotton. Beneath the swirling fog, the quiet forests luxuriate in the dampness — indeed, the great redwoods depend upon it as a condition of life itself.

16   NORTH COAST

QUIET RIVERS wind their way
through the redwood trees to the ocean. In
cathedral-like groves, the stately
trees soar above their forest companions and
form a canopy of branches high above
the ground. Once these giants filled a
forest 450 miles long, up to 30 miles wide,
and extending from the southwest
corner of Oregon to the Santa Lucia
Mountains south of Monterey. They grow
nowhere else in the world and are
one of the great scenic attractions
of California.

*BUILT BY YANKEES in the 1860's, Mendocino is a town where visitors from New England feel immediately at home. Escaping erasure by fire or improvement, it remains largely the way it looked in its prime, before the lumber industry moved away. Even the quaint figures of Father Time and the Maiden (*ABOVE RIGHT*), which cap the Masonic Hall, wear their years lightly.*

RICHARD DAWSON

RICHARD DAWSON

NORTH COAST   21

*T*HE OLD STOCKADES *of Fort Ross seem to echo to the ghostly footsteps of the Russian colonists who farmed, hunted, and traded here for twenty-nine years, from 1812 to 1841, in the service of the Czar.*

NORTH COAST 23

*THE WHITE BANKS AND CLIFFS described by Sir Francis Drake's
chaplain in 1579 may well have been these that rise at the shore of Drake's Bay in
a sheltering curve of the Point Reyes Peninsula. From the peninsula's tip, Point
Reyes Light sends forth its warnings to the ships of today from one of the foggiest
and windiest spots on the coast. Sea lions bask on the sandy beach below, ignoring
the winds, which sweep inland across the low, unprotected meadows of Point
Reyes National Seashore.*

24

NORTH COAST   25

THE NORTH BAY AREA

North of San Francisco, within the rain shadow of the Coast Range, lies a succession of pastoral valleys of quiet charm and open beauty. Every turn of the road reveals a vista of dozing vineyards, endless rows of truck crops, or orchards of pear, walnut, and apple trees. Great oaks and madrones march through the crops in ragged processions or gather in small groups in the open fields. Here and there, in pockets or on western slopes where the rain can reach them, are shady groves of conifers, strayed over the mountains from the heavily forested land to the west.

This beautiful land is at its best when the nip of fall is in the air. The hills flame with the fires of autumn, and a bright quilt of red, yellow, and amber spreads over the countryside. In this way the vineyards proclaim that the harvest is in, the grapes have been crushed, and the new year's wines are under way. The scent of smoldering leaves is overlaid with the heady bouquet of freshly crushed grapes and the astringent odor of raw wine in the first stages of processing.

The towns and cities, and the farming and resort communities, have a relaxed and settled air, and many of them are shaded by venerable elms that arch across the streets, forming long leafy tunnels.

Always a popular area for vacationers because of its natural, unpretentious beauty, its warm summer climate makes it especially alluring to fog-chilled San Franciscans, who flock to its resorts. The lakes, rivers, and the northern reaches of the Bay itself are usually thronged on weekends with fishermen, sail-boaters, and water-skiers.

The North Bay area reaches its southern limit in Marin County, one anchor of the Golden Gate Bridge and a bucolic contrast to the jampacked city across the strait. Marin is a pleasant residential area where almost every window looks out upon natural greenery and vistas of whitecapped water or up to the hazy summit of Mount Tamalpais, ancient guardian of the Bay. Within Marin's borders are spots of unforgettable beauty, including Muir Woods, an awe-inspiring stand of redwoods at the foot of Mount Tamalpais.

WINE INSTITUTE

APLIN-DUDLEY STUDIOS

NORTH BAY AREA   27

ACRES OF GRAPE VINES *stretch across rolling slopes and wide flatlands within the shadow of the purple hills that enclose the Napa Valley. In September and October, the heady aroma of newly crushed grapes fills the air, and the vineyards take on the bright gold and coppery red shades of autumn.*

NORTH BAY AREA　29

ROBERT THOMPSON

INSIDE PICTURESQUE WINERIES with thick walls and refreshingly cool rooms, huge containers of wood or steel or concrete hold the raw vintages during the months of aging. In proper time, the wine will be drawn off to produce the "bottled poetry" that captivated Robert Louis Stevenson when he sampled it more than eighty years ago.

BOB SMALLMAN

ABOVE THE WINE COUNTRY to the north lie higher valleys, and blue lakes encircled by low hills that are mantled with manzanita and oak. During much of the year the lakes are quiet, except on weekends when fishermen fill the boats tied on the shore of Upper Blue Lake (ABOVE) and brave the early-morning fog that sometimes blankets Clear Lake (RIGHT). In May, the summer throngs begin to fill the lakeside resorts and the lakes' surfaces become lively with swimmers, boaters, and water-skiers.

MIKE HAYDEN

NORTH BAY AREA 33

WAVES OF WHITE PETALS spread over apple orchards near
Sebastopol as spring brushes the land with color. Farther south, near the Golden
Gate, the still redwood groves of Muir Woods National Monument remain
cool and green no matter what the season. Now and then the sunlight finds an
opening in the luxuriant growth and slants down in shafts of dancing light.

ONE OF THE MOST DRAMATIC SIGHTS *in all California—the conquest
of San Francisco Bay by fog — can be witnessed from the top of Mount Tamalpais.
The fog builds up over the ocean and, seeking to overwhelm the warm valleys
behind the coastal mountains, it attacks the only opening in the range, the Golden
Gate. The rolling clouds quickly overrun the Gate and the city and send a long arm
stretching all the way across the bay to Berkeley.*

COLORFUL SAILS BILLOW before a spanking breeze, as threatening skies darken the Bay waters. In the distance, the bulky silhouette of Mount Tamalpais, crown of the North Bay's mountain system, dominates the view of the Marin Peninsula.

NORTH BAY AREA   39

40   NORTH BAY AREA

THE MARINE INFLUENCE is everywhere around horseshoe-shaped
Richardson Bay. Waterside communities are home ports for yachtsmen
and fishermen, havens for weary commuters, destinations for tourists, and
gathering places for artists. Off the Tiburon Peninsula, small craft glide
over the placid water of landlocked Belvedere Lagoon (ABOVE), and the
cliff-hanging community of Belvedere (LEFT) climbs up from the water's
edge. The view across Richardson Bay takes in the hilly shoreline of
the Marin Peninsula and the distant towers of the Golden Gate Bridge.

THE EAST BAY AREA

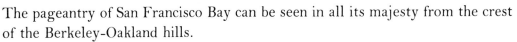

The pageantry of San Francisco Bay can be seen in all its majesty from the crest of the Berkeley-Oakland hills.

When rain clouds break up at sunset, the dome of heaven lights with the fires of the dying sun and the Bay mirrors them in molten splendor. On another day, fingers of fog may be seen stealing across from the Golden Gate, soon to be followed by swift cottony envelopment of the Bay and the hills as well. On a summer afternoon, the water reflects hot blinding sunlight back into the thousands of windows that face it, blinkered, shuttered, and louvered against the shimmering glare.

At night, the lights along the Bay shore twinkle in the misty darkness, and San Francisco glows with a pearly luminescence. The darkened Bay mirrors the sparkling lights of the cities along its rim and the topaz-spangled bridges that span it, and when the full moon rises, the water turns to polished silver.

This changeable pageant has attracted residents to the East Bay for nearly a century, and homes are tightly packed onto every view lot all the way up to the crest of the ridge, where they are stopped by the boundary of a regional park.

On the flatland at the foot of the range are beauty spots of less spectacular nature but of undisputed attraction. The campus of the University of California reflects in its sylvan repose the virtues of the classic plan upon which it has been developed. Architectural styles of different eras are happily absorbed in the groves of eucalyptus or isolated from each other by folds in the Berkeley hills.

Another man-made beauty spot, Oakland's Lake Merritt offers a restful retreat in a busy city. A wooded park surrounds the tidal inlet with landscaped promontories, leisurely walks, and jaunty little marinas.

On the other side of the ridge lies a contrasting world, drier, more open and less urbanized. It is a rolling pastoral countryside where shaded suburban settlements are interspersed among walnut groves, field crops, and dairy pastures. Farther to the east rises the sentinel of the East Bay, Mount Diablo, from whose summit more territory can be viewed than from any other point in the Bay Area.

KAISER GRAPHIC ARTS

ASUC GRAPHIC ARTS

JOHN ROBINSON

A BROODING BAY reflects the darkness of a stormy afternoon. Threatening clouds swirl above the bustling East Bay communities of Oakland, Berkeley, Alameda, Piedmont, Emeryville, and San Leandro as the glow of a fading sunset streaks the sky with pink above the Golden Gate.

44

EAST BAY AREA   45

LES FLOWERS, JR.

ABOVE THE CITIES, a wooded parkland, partly natural, partly man-made, runs along the crest of the East Bay ridge and spills over into the hilly country beyond. Lakes, reservoirs, and golf courses offer a respite from city pavements. Ducks float serenely on tiny, reed-rimmed Jewel Lake, and stands of eucalyptus trees send a sharp, fresh scent into the air.

GEORGE KNIGHT

A MOSAIC OF ROOFTOPS sweeps down the hillsides and across the flatland to the edge of the bay. At dusk, the lights of the East Bay communities twinkle like myriad diamonds against a backdrop of purple velvet, and the classic Campanile of the University of California at Berkeley (RIGHT) is a silver glow against a darkening sky. High up in the hills, astride the Oakland-Berkeley line, the venerable Claremont Hotel (ABOVE) has been a landmark since 1906.

48   EAST BAY AREA

FRANCES COLEBERD

A REFRESHING RETREAT
in Oakland's downtown area, 155-acre
Lake Merritt mirrors the hotels,
apartments, and office buildings
standing along a part of its shore.
Elsewhere around the lake, Oaklanders
come to stroll along tree-shaded
paths, relax in grassy parks, or to
feed the ducks in the wildfowl
refuge. On sunny weekends, dozens of
tiny sailboats ripple the lake's surface.

EAST BAY AREA 51

*BEHIND THE HILLS lies a peaceful, slow-paced countryside. In the
shadow of Mount Diablo, roads meander casually between rolling pastures and hilly
fields dotted with native oaks and chaparral. From the summit of the mountain,
on a sparkling clear day, the view takes in thirty-five counties, and mountain peaks
from Mount Shasta to the Tehachapis. A dry land, this region enjoys a few weeks
of emerald green following the winter rains, then becomes a soft carpet of rich
golden brown for the rest of the year.*

52

EAST BAY AREA 53

SAN FRANCISCO

No city in California—and few in the world—can equal the scenic beauty of San Francisco. Built on the hilly tip of a peninsula, its uneven terrain gives it unique three-dimensional form. A city of many moods, induced by the hourly changes of weather, it may glisten in sparkling sunshine, its cubical buildings distinctly delineated in the clear air; or it may lie partly swathed in cloud shadow and partly exposed in bright sunlight; or, fog may steal across, casting a thin veil between one neighborhood and the next or flowing down off the hills to obliterate everything in sight.

The hills open countless vistas of rollercoaster streets, swooping up and down; of the jaunty little cable cars clambering up the rises; of patches of the Bay, the East Bay hills, or the green shores of Marin, viewed at the end of long defiles of close-packed buildings.

A port city, its harbor is visited by a procession of freighters and ocean liners. White, black, and rusty red, flying the colors of every nation, they pass through the Golden Gate and come gingerly to berth at the Embarcadero. Lean fighting ships pass under the bridge, their decks packed with white-hatted sailors, momentarily marveling at the grandeur of the city while they restlessly await their shore passes.

To the north and east, the great bridges hang over the water, suspended from heavy steel cables, monuments to the imagination and daring of the men who dreamed them into reality. The orange towers of the Golden Gate Bridge are often shrouded in the fog that funnels through the slot, sometimes high enough to erase the tops of the towers, sometimes pouring through like a river just under the roadway, and sometimes engulfing everything in blinding mist. The majestic Bay Bridge, less spectacularly sited than its companion, compensates by the grand scale of its soaring leap across the wide Bay.

Once a dozing Spanish village, San Francisco became the emporium of a new world when the Gold Rush exploded in its midst. Overnight, the little settlement grew into a boisterous, frenetic metropolis. The energy that the venturesome Fortyniners and their successors poured into the city gave it a head start over the others on the coast. It grew and prospered, suffered the catastrophic fire and earthquake of 1906, and recovered to continue its growth. Few relics of the early days have survived the fire or the needs of civic growth, but the Gold Rush energy lingers in a shadowy form, nurtured by a stimulating climate and an inspirational setting.

RICHARD DAWSON

DAVE HARTLEY

GLENN CHRISTIANSEN

FROM THE TOP OF TWIN PEAKS, the white, magic city of San Francisco spreads out before the eye. In the foreground, tightly packed houses crowd the hillside, and beyond them, the tall structures of the downtown area rise like castle towers.

SAN FRANCISCO　57

INTO THE PORT OF SAN FRANCISCO come vessels from all over the world, sailing beneath the graceful span of the Golden Gate Bridge with their cargoes of coffee, tea, and spices, cameras and stainless steel, furniture and sports cars. As the holds of the ships are emptied onto the docks, they are refilled with cotton, wine, oranges, frozen foods, cement, wheat, rice, and olive oil from the fields and factories of California.

*BRIGHT SPLASHES OF COLOR contribute a cheery note in the
midst of the downtown bustle. Gay sidewalk flower stands reflect the
seasons in their changing displays—perky narcissus in spring, tiny rosebuds
in summer, chrysanthemums in fall, holly in winter. At Powell and
Geary streets, the flowers frame a view of the fashionable St. Francis
Hotel (*LEFT*). On busy Market Street, the plaza of the Standard Oil
Company building is an island of quiet beauty, where the refreshing sound
of splashing water is combined with restful greenery and masses of blooms.*

SAN FRANCISCO   61

A STEEP CLIMB up California Street, made easier by jaunty little cable cars, brings a change from the canyons of commerce below to the airy heights of Nob Hill. Near Grant Avenue, California Street crosses the southern reaches of San Francisco's Chinatown, where the roll of drums annually heralds the approach of the colorful Chinese New Year parade.

A WHITE, BILLOWING FOG, driven inland by a stiff salt breeze,
swirls across the hilltops of the city and envelops the rows of houses in
its chill dampness. On a winter evening, the plane trees atop Nob Hill
(RIGHT) are pleached and leafless, and the fog blurs the outline of Grace
Cathedral. On a night like this, the air is fresh, and the pedestrians move
at a brisk pace along the fog-slick sidewalk.

*IN CLOSED RANKS, the houses march straight up the hillside, obedient
to the regimented street system applied to most of the city's forty hills.
The homes huddle together on their narrow lots, their windows faced toward
the view and the morning sun. In the background, behind a gauzelike
curtain of fog, the towers of the business district await their turn in the sun.
On Telegraph Hill (LEFT), the houses cling tenaciously to ledges in the
cliffside below Coit Tower, hanging on desperately to preserve a view that is
well worth the daily ascent of endless flights of steep steps.*

SAN FRANCISCO **67**

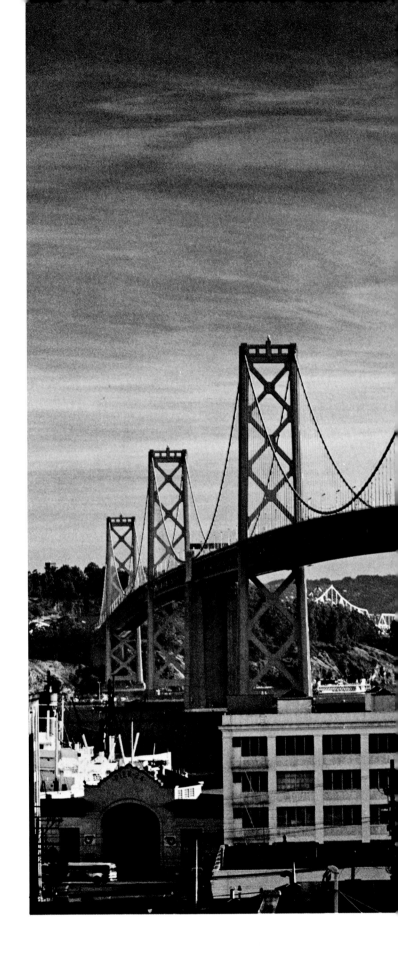

SPANNING THE WATERS of the bay, the San Francisco-Oakland Bay Bridge speeds commuters back and forth between the cities on the east and west shores. The bridge and its approaches stretch for eight miles. Midway on its journey, the roadway tunnels through the rocky mass of Yerba Buena Island, called Goat Island in the days of the Forty-niners when hundreds of the animals roamed the grassy slopes.

SAN FRANCISCO   69

GEORGE KNIGHT

AT GHIRARDELLI SQUARE,
the old red brick buildings of a former
chocolate factory wear a new face.
Tourists and San Franciscans flock to
restaurants and shops, art galleries
and craft museums. From the deck
overlooking the landscaped plaza, the
view is north across Victorian Park to
the ship museum at Hyde Street
Pier, and beyond to now-deserted
Alcatraz Island. A few blocks away,
San Francisco's fishing fleet is berthed
at Fisherman's Wharf (ABOVE) *as it*
has been since the city's early days,
and at Wharf restaurants, thousands
of visitors sample the catch.

DOROTHY KRELL

BEYOND THE WOODED ACRES of the Army's Presidio (LEFT), *a cluster of high-rise apartments looks down from Russian Hill. Just outside the Presidio gate, the restored Palace of Fine Arts* (ABOVE), *built for the Panama-Pacific International Exposition of 1915, occupies a lovely setting alongside a quiet lagoon.*

SAN FRANCISCO   73

GEORGE KNIGHT

74   SAN FRANCISCO

GEORGE KNIGHT

IN GOLDEN GATE PARK, the delightfully Victorian conservatory is a replica of the Royal Conservatory in Kew Gardens, England. Inside, in the humid atmosphere, the plants on display are lush and tropical. Outside, the beds glow with ever-changing plantings of colorful annuals. Elsewhere in the park, autumn brings splashes of red and yellow to the garden plantings in the Japanese Tea Garden (ABOVE). *In early April, the fragile blossoms of the garden's 200 cherry trees are at their peak.*

IN A BEAUTIFUL SETTING in Lincoln Park, overlooking a magnificent vista of the Golden Gate, the California Palace of the Legion of Honor is a dignified memorial to the California soldiers who gave their lives during World War 1. The museum is a replica of the Palais de la Legion d'Honneur in Paris. Within its rooms is a superb collection of French art and furniture, including forty Rodin bronzes.

SAN FRANCISCO   77

GLENN CHRISTIANSEN

UNDER FULL SAIL, racing yachts skim over the whitecaps just inside the Golden Gate, taking advantage of a brisk 20-knot wind pouring through the narrow strait. A paradise for skilled yachtsmen, the bay tests their seamanship with its strong winds and powerful tides. In a quieter vein, sunworshippers dot the wide beach that runs for three miles alongside the Great Highway at the western edge of the city.

THE PENINSULA AND SOUTH BAY AREA

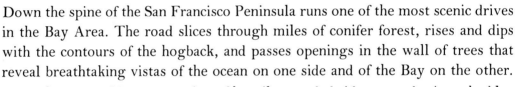

Down the spine of the San Francisco Peninsula runs one of the most scenic drives in the Bay Area. The road slices through miles of conifer forest, rises and dips with the contours of the hogback, and passes openings in the wall of trees that reveal breathtaking vistas of the ocean on one side and of the Bay on the other.

On the ocean side, a succession of heavily-wooded ridges recedes into the blue distance, melting into the shimmering sea. Few signs of human habitation are visible: an occasional roadhouse, a plume of smoke from a cabin chimney, or a dirt road disappearing into the pines.

To the east, the forest drops abruptly away to a wide shelf, solidly checkerboarded with streets and buildings, that spreads to the edge of the Bay. Beyond is the sparkling silver of the water and beyond that are the dry hills of the opposite shore.

The wooded western half is a place to play, and visitors throng its forested parks and swimming beaches. Along the rocky coastline, scores of doughty fishermen cast into the surf from perilous perches on the spume-flecked rocks.

The eastern half is a place to live, and its shaded streets are lined with pleasant homes and verdant gardens aglow with floral color. Heart of the area is the 8,800-acre campus of Stanford University, a refreshing pastoral island in a sea of residential and commercial envelopment.

At the base of the Peninsula and below the marshy tip of the Bay, a long and fertile valley stretches for many level miles between flanking mountain ranges. In spring, the valley bursts out in waves of pink, as the orchards unfurl their blossoms, or in miles of rich brown earth, freshly furrowed for the truck crops that are to come. Atop the accompanying mountains, the silvery domes of Lick Observatory can be seen to sparkle when the sun strikes them. Farther south, the jumbled rocks of Pinnacles National Monument attract the curious because of their fantastic domes, spires, caverns, and tunnels.

MARTIN LITTON

KARL OBERT

RICHARD DAWSON

SOUTH BAY AREA   81

THE BUFF SANDSTONE BUILDINGS of Stanford University
(RIGHT) *have long been one of the Peninsula's major attractions. Most famous*
of the university's many features is the striking Venetian mosaic of the
Sermon on the Mount that glows on the façade of the beautiful Memorial
Church. Not far from the university, the gardens of Sunset Magazine
(ABOVE) *are a showplace for trees, shrubs, and flowers from all sections of*
the Pacific Coast and offer displays of blossoms that change with the seasons.

A HAPPY COMBINATION of architecture, landscaping, and site, the distinctive campus of Foothill College spreads over a traffic-free hillside in Los Altos Hills. The rolling hills that form a backdrop for the hipped shake roofs change with the seasons from rich green to tawny gold. In spring, nearby apricot, almond, pear, and prune orchards burst forth in a showy froth of blossoms, here and there set off against a bright carpet of yellow mustard.

FOOTHILL COLLEGE

RICHARD BROOKS

86 SOUTH BAY AREA

*ROLLING HILLSIDES, lush and
green after the winter's rains, form a restful
backdrop for the teeming cities of the
Peninsula. A landmark of the area is the
Pulgas Water Temple, at the southern tip of
Crystal Springs Reservoir. Its calm reflecting
pool is in sharp contrast to the dramatically
surging waters which rush through
the well of the temple at the end of their
162-mile journey from Yosemite National Park.*

SOUTH BAY AREA   87

THE MIND FINDS PEACE within the boundaries of state redwood parks
near Santa Cruz. Magnificent groves of coast redwoods are protected here, and
soft light filters down through interlacing branches of madrone, alder,
maple, oak, and laurel. Delicate ferns thrive in deeply shaded glades.
At left, a silvery veil of water cascades over a rocky bank in Big Basin
park. In Henry Cowell park above, a sun-dappled path leads two young
visitors beneath a lacy canopy into the darker depths of the redwood forest.

SOUTH BAY AREA   89

A WARMING BLANKET of polyethylene strips, put down in February,
gives strawberry plants in the Salinas Valley a head start on the growing season.
The roots thrive beneath the glistening cover, and by late April, the first
luscious berries will await the pickers.

90

AL WEBER

SOUTH BAY AREA   91

92   SOUTH BAY AREA

AL WEBER

*THE CLOISTERED COLONNADE of
San Juan Bautista's mission seems to echo the
footsteps of the Franciscan Fathers, and the
carefully restored buildings around the mission
Plaza seem to await the arrival of the passengers who
will climb wearily down from the Concord stage.
The mission still serves its predominantly Spanish-
speaking parish, but the last of the stages rattled
down the Old Stage Road and came to an abrupt
stop before the Plaza Hotel in 1872.*

IRRIGATED FIELDS replace the wild oats and yellow mustard that once grew tall in the lower reaches of the Salinas Valley. The rounded, velvety hills of the Gabilan Range on the horizon contrast sharply with the incredibly jumbled spires and crags of the Pinnacles (RIGHT) which rear into the sky a short distance away, an impressive reminder of volcanic eruptions millions of years ago.

RICHARD DAWSON

THE CENTRAL COAST

The Central Coast, stretching from Monterey to Morro Bay, runs a gamut from crowded seaside resorts to empty miles of nothingness, from smooth accessible beaches to tall cliffs that drop straight down into the sea, and from dark-forested mountains to desert-like hills dotted with yuccas.

"The one common note of all this country," observed Robert Louis Stevenson, "is the haunting presence of the ocean. Everywhere, even in quiet weather, the low, distant, thrilling roar of the Pacific hangs over the coast and the adjacent country like smoke above the battle."

The call of the ocean draws people to this beautiful coast to swim in the chilly surf, perhaps to sun in the tangy air, or simply to take in the unspoiled beauty of the white beaches spreading at the base of the dark, menacing forests.

Offshore, flocks of screeching gulls wheel and dive for food carried on the tide or smashed out of rocky sanctuaries by the waves. Sea lions, matted together on the rocks, call out in stentorian bellows that can be heard above the roar of the breakers.

At the northern end of this coastal province, the city of Monterey spreads along the shore of a crescent-shaped harbor, edged with piers, canneries, and restaurants and populated with fishing boats that come and go with an air of self-importance.

Ever since its curving bay was discovered and claimed for the King of Spain by Cabrillo in 1542, Monterey has been a fixture in the history of California. A scattering of restored adobes reminds the visitor of the proud days when it was the capital of Spanish Alta California and the center of a colorful social and political swirl that lasted for 70 eventful years, from 1775 to 1846.

Around the square-shaped Monterey Peninsula, a scenic road winds past neatly groomed estates, golf courses, and resorts to reach Carmel-by-the-Sea, a picturesque town founded in 1915 by a group of artists and writers and still vigorously defending its individualism against the encroachments of commerce. Beyond Carmel, the coast runs past spectacular Big Sur and then takes off on the lonely and dramatic 125 miles to Morro Bay.

RICHARD DAWSON

RICHARD DAWSON

CLYDE CHILDRESS

OLD SPANISH CAPITAL and *cradle of California history, Monterey is one of the best documented of American towns. Flags of the federal government and the state of California fly above Colton Hall* (LEFT), *where California's Constitutional Convention met in 1849. The Old Whaling Station* (ABOVE), *built in 1855, served as a boarding house for Portuguese whalers who operated for two decades in the waters between California and Hawaii.*

MAGNIFICENTLY UNSPOILED and dramatically beautiful, the coastline of Del Monte Forest is one of the most spectacular stretches of seacoast in the world. In this setting of tremendous, sparkling scenery, five world-famous courses challenge golfers. Offshore, brisk ocean breezes send boats skimming over dancing waves.

100   CENTRAL COAST

CENTRAL COAST 101

*IN A PEACEFUL SETTING near sea and mountains, the lovely
Carmel Mission, headquarters for the California mission chain from 1770
to 1803, is a fitting resting place for Father Junipero Serra, founder of the
missions. The mellow sandstone walls, rebuilt after decades of neglect,
look much as they did when the mission was a flourishing center surrounded
by orchards, cattle and sheep range, and fields of crops. The nearby
countryside is pastoral still. Cattle graze on green hillsides near Point
Lobos, and fields of artichokes thrive in the moist coastal air.*

102

DAVID MUENCH

A LONG CRESCENT of white powdery sand, edged with pine and cypress, curves alongside the sparkling waters of Carmel Bay. A bright spot of green marks the famed Pebble Beach Golf Links, and far off in the distance, forming the southern headland of the bay, rugged Point Lobos reaches a long arm out from the shadowy hills of the Santa Lucia Range. In the lonely mountains to the south, an occasional chill fog gathers under the slanting rays of a late afternoon sun and rolls down the hillside to the sea.

CENTRAL COAST   105

THE STRUGGLE FOR SURVIVAL rages along the coast under conditions of haunting beauty. Screaming seagulls wheel and dive above the boiling surf off Point Lobos, seeking the marine animals carried by the incoming tide or dislodged from their rocky refuges by the smash of the waves. A twisted cypress, silhouetted against a painted sky, seems to be resting between rounds in its eternal bout with the wind.

DAVID MUENCH

108   CENTRAL COAST

A RESTLESS SURF plays against the rocky shore south of Carmel. Not far away, in the lovely rolling countryside of Carmel Valley (ABOVE), *Father Serra's mission cattle once grazed on peaceful slopes and rancheros led a life of leisure on old Spanish land grants. Cattle still roam on Valley ranches, and the chaparral-crowned uplands still hide deer, rabbits, coyotes, and wild boar, but the Valley today is also a place of attractive homes and resorts, luxurious retirement communities, and handsome shopping centers.*

*THIS BEAUTIFUL LAND is littered with melancholy monuments to men's attempts to wrest a living from the rocky soil. A forlorn ranch house, framed in the skeletal branches of a wind-torn tree, epitomizes the struggle that more than one family has endured in an attempt to live in isolation. But while men come and go, the native plants live on and on. A luxuriant growth of stonecrop (*ABOVE*) draws sustenance from the trunks of long-dead cypresses.*

CENTRAL COAST   111

A FAIRYTALE CASTLE rises atop La Cuesta (The Enchanted Hill) above San Simeon. La Casa Grande dominates the scene with its cathedral-like façade and twin bell towers of Spanish Renaissance design. This was once the headquarters of the late William Randolph Hearst. Lavishly furnished with priceless art objects, surrounded by terraced gardens, and backed by the imposing Santa Lucia Mountains, the fabulous estate is now a state park, open to the public.

112

SANTA BARBARA

In 1786 an altar candle was lit at the dedication of Mission Santa Barbara. To-day, this flame is still burning, having never once been snuffed out. In a sense, this continuous speck of light symbolizes Santa Barbara itself, for alone of all the major California cities, it has been able to keep alive a vital connection with its Spanish heritage.

The Spanish motif is plainly discernible throughout the city. In addition to a dozen lovingly restored adobes and the impressive Mission itself, a number of Spanish-style homes, shops, and civic structures perpetuate the Hispanic architecture in latter-day form. Spanish street names—De la Guerra, Carrillo, Cañon Perdido, Indio Muerto—memorialize pioneer families or events that occurred in early days. And every August, when the full moon sails over the bay, the city turns back the years and revisits its romantic past for several days of spirited and colorful pageantry.

For nearly a century after its founding in 1782, Santa Barbara enjoyed a re-laxed and prosperous existence. Land holding families, grown wealthy from the hide-and-tallow trade, maintained townhouses where they carried on a courtly and hospitable way of life. It was a leisurely life, with plenty of time for fiestas and fandangos, bull and bear fights, horse racing, and costumed cavalcades that swept over the countryside to visit the ranchos. In time, the pastoral idyl ended; but many of the *rancheros* stayed on, carrying forward the old traditions as best they could. Some of the city's first families today are directly descended from these proud *Barbareños*.

The beautiful natural setting, which attracted the original Spanish colonists and later settlers as well, is a tree-shaded, hilly plain that lies between the back-drop of the sheer Santa Ynez Mountains and the shore of a gently curving bay. Spread over the irregular terrain, the city's verdant gardens and gracious homes convey an air of spaciousness and quiet comfort. Along the waterfront, a broad palm-lined esplanade runs from a still lagoon, where waterfowl live in open sanctuary, to a busy yacht basin, where white boats bob up and down with the rhythm of the tide.

Over the crest of the Santa Ynez range, a world of rolling ranchland spreads over the oak-shaded hills where vaqueros once raced after gawky, long-horned cattle or lassoed grizzlies for harassment at the next fiesta.

MARTIN LITTON

MARTIN LITTON

BOLD AND COLORFUL and richly ornamented, Santa Barbara's
rambling Spanish-style courthouse has been described as the most beautiful
civic building in the country. Everything about it is on a lavish scale: the
imposing arched entryway; the decorated interior walls of the clock
tower which rise several stories to a frescoed ceiling; the intricately wrought
ironwork that carried the Spanish motif to every corner of the great
building. Much of the furniture is handmade, and every piece is in complete
harmony with its setting.

116

*UNDER A FULL MOON, a ghost fleet rides at anchor on the dark waters
of the harbor. A mixture of pleasure craft and fishing vessels takes shelter
here, bobbing restlessly to the slap of the wavelets. Soon, the harbor will
awaken and the fishing boats will chug out to sea. Then the populace will
begin to stir, and the first visitor of the day will stroll the hard-packed sand.*

SANTA BARBARA   119

A TRADITION-MINDED CITY, Santa Barbara displays its
appreciation of its Spanish heritage in various ways. Shoppers stroll through
a pleasant shaded street of Spanish-style stores, which front on a flagstone
passageway as narrow as a village street in Spain. During the three
nights of the full moon in August, residents celebrate a re-creation of the
old Spanish days. Costumed horsemen on richly caparisoned Palominos ride
in the colorful parade that is the main feature of the festival.

THE QUEEN OF THE MISSIONS stands as an impressive monument to the devotion, skill, and energy of the handful of padres who were able to create the massive structure in 1815 from simple materials at hand, with few tools, and with the help of unskilled Indians. The blend of Spanish-Moorish architecture is graced by a classic façade, derived from a design in a first-century book on architecture written by a Roman scholar.

JOSEF MUENCH

A SPRINGTIME SPECTACLE occurs northwest of Santa Barbara when Lompoc's 2,500 acres of commercial flower fields burst into bloom. Row after row of sweet peas, poppies, calendulas, nasturtiums, and larkspurs turn the landscape into a rainbow of red, purple, gold, orange, yellow, blue, and white. Just north of the city, the afternoon sun casts long shadows over the quiet hills of San Marcos Pass, gateway to the far-flung ranch country behind Santa Barbara.

SANTA BARBARA   125

THE SOUTH COAST

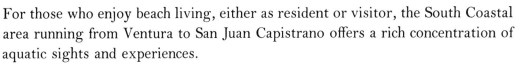

For those who enjoy beach living, either as resident or visitor, the South Coastal area running from Ventura to San Juan Capistrano offers a rich concentration of aquatic sights and experiences.

For many miles, the coastal shelf slopes so gradually into the sea that the wide expanses of sandy beach slow the rolling surf to a gentle, lacy swirl. Cliffs and rocks are in abundance, but they do not dominate the shoreline, and the miles of open strand are easily accessible. A warm ocean current, running south from Point Conception, tempers the surf to an agreeable mildness; and though fogs and mist occasionally roll in off the ocean, the sky is usually clear and the salty air is soft and balmy.

The coastal strip offers a variety of scenic vistas. At its northern end, a forest of derricks stands in the pounding surf, serenely pumping oil from deep in the earth, oblivious to the surge of the tides. A wide highway sweeps along the shore almost at sea level, running a gauntlet between the thundering surf and tall cliffs that seem to teeter overhead. All along the way, homes are built as close to the sea as possible, some on the sand just beyond the reach of the highest tide and some on the bluffs above, jumbled closely together, each seeking the most advantageous view of the Pacific. In the sheltered channels offshore, small boats trace busy patterns in the blue water that separates the mainland from a scattering of island beach colonies.

An arid land, its open hills and fields are either matted with chaparral or covered with wild grass that is scorched brown in summer. Most of the verdure has been introduced by man. The headlands and inland valleys are greened over with irrigated fields of beans, tomatoes, and alfalfa, boxed in by tall eucalyptus windbreaks. In the beach towns, files of spindly, mop-headed palms rise into the sky, marking the course of the streets or the presence of a shopping center. The gardens glow with subtropical blossoms set off by large-leafed shrubs; and here and there, flashes of incandescent magenta and pink signal the presence of bougainvillea or ice plant, whose intense colors rival the brilliance of the sun.

WILLIAM APLIN

DAVID MUENCH

GLENN CHRISTIANSEN

THE LONG CURVING SHORE of Santa Monica Bay twinkles
with lights from the houses, apartments, and hotels that cluster along it.
A string of lights on the distant horizon marks the Palos Verdes
Peninsula, the southern headland of the bay. West of Santa Monica,
Mediterranean-style houses cling to the bluffs at Malibu (RIGHT). *Below*
them, between the cliffs and the pounding surf, a broad highway follows the
jagged shoreline into the hazy distance.

BUILT ON A PROMONTORY in Palos Verdes, the unique little Wayfarers' Chapel designed by Lloyd Wright welcomes all faiths to meditate and worship within its luminous walls of glass. Off Palos Verdes Point, waves wash over the battered hulk of the freighter Dominator, *stranded here on March 15, 1961. The wreck still survives, but the pounding seas continue to wear it down and its days are doubtlessly numbered.*

SOUTH COAST   131

CORE OF A PLANNED COMMUNITY, the 1,000-acre campus of the University of California at Irvine is being developed within a master plan for 10,000 acres of former cattle range. The heart of the plan is the university campus. Surrounding and blending with it is a community that is planned eventually to have 100,000 residents. Not far from the academic world of the campus, the breakers off the south coast beaches lure both expert and amateur, and a variety of waterworld activities brings crowds to enjoy the sun, the sand, and the sea.

THE MOODS OF THE OCEAN change from hour to hour. Under the light of a full moon, Laguna Beach takes on an air of romance, of mystery, and of tranquility. In a different mood, the waves of daytime challenge the man of action to pit his skills against the denizens of the tides and to taste the dangers of the smashing surf.

SAFE ANCHORAGE in sheltered bays and salt-water channels brings thousands of pleasure craft to south coast waters. On summer weekends, the basins are lively with boats of every description, from the smallest rowboat to the largest yacht. Sails billow before gentle winds, and skippers test their nautical knowledge on the rippled waters of Newport Bay Harbor (ABOVE), Long Beach Harbor (RIGHT), and other protected inlets.

THE STATELY RUINS of Mission San Juan Capistrano seem to echo to the ghostly footfalls of the padres and Indians who worshipped and labored here for the brief years of its life. One of the most beautiful of the California missions, the massive structure was largely destroyed by an earthquake in 1812, a scant six years after its completion. It has never completely recovered. The standing arcades still show the scars of the quake. Only unscathed link with the past is the richly ornamented, gold-leafed altar.

138   SOUTH COAST

OFFSHORE ISLANDS tantalize land-bound observers on clear days. Their protected coves offer shelter for yachtsmen, and crystal-clear waters draw fishermen, swimmers, and underwater explorers. Santa Cruz Island (LEFT) is the largest island off the coast of California. Once a Mexican penal colony, it is now grazing land for cattle and sheep. Farther south, small boats gather in Avalon Bay (ABOVE), the beautiful harbor of Santa Catalina Island. Behind the bay, the homes, resorts, and shops of the town of Avalon climb chaparral-covered hillsides.

LOS ANGELES

The great, sprawling city of Los Angeles spreads over a dry alluvial plain that fans out from the base of the mountains and runs to the sea. Naturally flat, the site offers few elevated vantage points and little relief from the grand monotony of its sweep. Here and there a chain of hills plows into the sea of buildings, or a wooded, dry watercourse meanders through, but in general the structural ocean spreads without hindrance or relief in all directions.

Viewed from above, this prairie of buildings takes on an amazing transformation. A raw, pulsing vitality seems to rise from the massed structures. The audacious freeways flow through the city, weaving, crossing, and blending together like themes in a musical score. From the heights, even the smog acquires a perverse beauty as it veils parts of the city from sight. At night, the horizonless sweep of the lights outshines the starlit heavens with its geometric constellations and clusters of auroral color where the neon gathers.

Most of the elements of grace and beauty within the city are man-made and are scattered over a broad canvas. Sylvan parks, graced with lakes and bright subtropical plantings, landscaped grounds of museums and art galleries, and verdant campuses bring oases of graceful verdure into the heart of the metropolis.

Architecturally, the city displays a venturesome creativity that adds luster to the prospect. Hillside and canyon residential areas reveal progressive and imaginative home designs and landscaping practices. Broad boulevards, most notably Wilshire, run for miles through canyons of fresh, attractive business structures designed with taste and restraint.

The influence of Hollywood may show up here and there in flamboyant night club and restaurant façades, but at its best, it produces delightful surprises, such as the bits of Disneyland that charm the eye with flashes of nostalgic beauty.

Like most of Southern California, Los Angeles is more interested in today than yesterday, and the picturesque relics of its colorful history are nearly submerged in the metropolitan sweep. However, two imposing missions, a restoration of the original Spanish plaza, and a scattering of fine museums provide an illuminating glimpse into the city's heritage.

On the outskirts of the city, a mountain playground swings around the northeastern periphery and a lively water-world along the western edge. Both of these are treated in separate chapters.

BARRY ANDERSON

WELTON BECKET AND ASSOCIATES

DAVID MUENCH

LOS ANGELES   143

THE CITY SPARKLES when night falls. The strains of a symphony float over the hills of Hollywood from the great shell in Hollywood Bowl, and an audience of some 20,000 music lovers sits in rapt attention. In the distance, traffic courses over a freeway, lights twinkle in hillside homes, and the Los Angeles basin glows with star-spangled activity. From the heights above Griffith Observatory, the lights present a fascinating and changeable spectacle, like an orderly reflection of the starry sky itself.

DAVID MUENCH

*FRESH AND IMAGINATIVE architectural design, inviting
landscaping, and bold city planning are bringing a new look to many parts
of the city. Opulent Wilshire Boulevard (ABOVE) conveys an impression
of uncrowded spaciousness despite the prodigious volume of traffic and the
office buildings, department stores, hotels, and apartments that line its
sixteen miles. In the heart of downtown, the city's Civic Center (RIGHT) is
an impressive progression of buildings surrounding a landscaped mall. At
one end, overlooking fountains and reflecting pools, the dramatic Water
and Power Building, always fully lighted at night, towers above the
handsome theaters of the Music Center.*

A BEAUTIFUL SHOWCASE
for art, the four-story Ahmanson
Gallery seems to float above the
reflecting pool of the grand entry.
One of three buildings in the Los
Angeles Museum of Art complex, the
Ahmanson Gallery contains the
museum's permanent art collections.
The other two pavilions house
changing displays, a theater,
restaurant, art rentals, and children's
art galleries.

148

JULIUS SHULMAN

WOODED PARKS are welcome oases on the doorsteps of downtown.
Wide, paved paths wind through the thirty acres of Lacy Park (ABOVE) in
San Marino, and rare Montezuma cypresses cast cooling shadows. In
Elysian Park (RIGHT), California native palms stand out against a
eucalyptus forest background in Chavez Ravine Arboretum. This was the first
botanical garden in Southern California, launched by the Los Angeles
Horticultural Society in 1893. It contains plants from all over the world.

THE PATTERNS OF THE CITY are varied. High-rise buildings reach for the sky in the business districts. They fill the center of the V formed by the intersection of Wilshire and Santa Monica boulevards (RIGHT) and line both sides of Wilshire Boulevard, which reaches out to the horizon. In outlying residential areas, the pattern is a carpet of rooftops laced with winding streets.

LOS ANGELES   153

DOROTHY KRELL

THE GIANT CAMPUS of the University of California at Los Angeles spreads over 411 acres of terraced foothills off Sunset Boulevard. Early campus buildings of imposing Romanesque design contrast sharply with the smooth, many-windowed façades of the modern buildings that are part of the very extensive building program that has been under way on the campus since the end of World War II.

LOS ANGELES 155

156   LOS ANGELES

FLAGS OF THE NATIONS
represented among the student body fly beneath the
graceful arches of the Von KleinSmid Center of
International and Public Affairs on the campus of
the University of Southern California. A nighttime
view through one of the archways frames the
12-story Waite Phillips Hall of Education.

GREAT TRAFFIC ARTERIES carry the life blood of the sprawling city from its heart to its farthest extremities. At night the freeways become rivers of light, carrying a pulsing flow of tens of thousands of vehicles to and from the business core of the city.

LOS ANGELES   159

TWO PASADENA LANDMARKS are the impressive, domed City
Hall, hub of a 1923 plan for a formal civic center, and the famous Rose
Bowl, where major western and eastern college teams have played their
annual New Year's Day football classic since 1902. The huge bowl stands
on the outskirts of the city in Brookside Park, flanked on both sides by
wooded residential areas graced with fine homes and beautiful gardens and
backed by the purple-shadowed San Gabriel Mountains.

IN A DIGNIFIED SETTING behind the pillared façade of the Henry E. Huntington Library in San Marino, more than two million treasured books and manuscripts are preserved for use by scholars from all over the world, and many precious volumes are on permanent display. A famed collection of paintings is housed in the nearby Art Gallery, and one of the world's great botanical gardens spreads over 207 surrounding acres. The Desert Garden (RIGHT) contains the largest collection of mature specimens of cacti and other succulents in the world.

LOS ANGELES 163

*A RICHLY DECORATED ALTAR glows in the muted light within
the Mission San Gabriel* (1771). *Painted and gilded figures of the
saints, elaborate scrolls, and other religious ornaments show the firm but
unschooled hand of the Indian craftsmen who fashioned them. The bells of
San Gabriel hang in a picturesque campanario which replaced a tower that
toppled in the earthquake of 1812.*

LOS ANGELES   165

ROBERT GARRICK ASSOCIATES

*AFOOT OR AFLOAT, visitors delight in meandering about the uniquely landscaped Busch Gardens (*ABOVE*) in the San Fernando Valley. An unexpected sight on the flat Valley scene, the park has tropical and mountain landscapes linked by pleasant waterways that encircle handsome refreshment pavilions. At Descanso Gardens (*RIGHT*) in La Canada, tea is served beneath the blue tile roof of a tea pavilion set among native oaks in an Oriental garden noted for its beautiful plantings of camellias and azaleas.*

INDIAN DESIGNS and Spanish motifs are blended in the cool, musty chapel of the San Fernando Mission. Founded in 1797, the mission prospered for forty years and then fell into disuse for a century. Now restored, it has an air of simple dignity, peacefulness, and quiet charm.

168   LOS ANGELES

A FAIRYTALE WORLD of the past and the streamlined world of today turn up in delightful form at Disneyland. The pinnacled castle of Sleeping Beauty seems to echo to the clank of armor, the sighs of imprisoned maidens, and the snorts of circling dragons. Not far away, the transportation of tomorrow whisks passengers silently over a concrete highway in the sky, high above a surfacing submarine on a lagoon in Tomorrowland. In the background, bobsleds race down the precipitous sides of the Matterhorn.

SAN DIEGO

Blessed by a genial climate that encourages outdoor living all through the year, San Diegans concentrate with enthusiasm on the enjoyment of an idyllic water-world that embraces a magnificent landlocked harbor and a limitless strand of silvery beaches.

The quiet waters of the bay, protected from the ocean's surges by natural breakwaters, provide shelter for a melange of vessels of all sizes and shapes. Hosts of small pleasure craft cut frisky wakes among the monsters of ocean commerce and a conglomeration of dark gray navy ships anchored in the bay or cruising majestically through the blue water. Along the bayshore, hundreds of moth-balled fighting ships are moored together in tight packs, hull to hull.

Along the ocean shore, a series of white bathing beaches runs for 30-odd miles from Del Mar almost to the Mexican border. Here, under the ever-azure sky, thousands of swimmers come to ride the tepid breakers or to sun on the sand. In Mission Bay Park—an immense inland extension of the ocean playground—waterskiers, multicolored sails, and excursion boats pass to and fro in a lively minuet.

Not all of it open beach, the coastline presents a variety of scenic sights. The intricate, lacy patterns eroded into the cliffs of Torrey Pines Mesa look like giant shawls dropping down into the water. At La Jolla, the surf swirls among the rocks of a sheltered bathing cove; and at high-high tide, the breakers smash against the cliffs in towering explosions of spray. Farther south, the long, high promontory of Point Loma stretches a protecting arm across the entrance to the bay and offers from its heights an unequaled view of the city and the shimmering Pacific.

A very different kind of attraction, verdant Balboa Park spreads its 1,400 acres of landscaped arroyos and mesas in a veritable Forest of Arden in the heart of the city. Some of the old rococo buildings of the exposition of 1915 still stand amid immaculately kept grounds, shaded by tall, blue-green eucalyptus trees. Not the least of the park's attractions is the picturesque zoo, where the denizens prowl in natural grottoes.

A pastoral, unspoiled back country lies to the east of the city. The old Mission, first in the California chain (1774), stands in dignified decay in a quiet valley. Beyond, a series of farming valleys recedes to the east, giving way eventually to pine-shadowed mountains that drop off abruptly to the silvery sink of the Imperial Valley a mile straight down.

CITY OF SAN DIEGO

DOROTHY KRELL

DOROTHY KRELL

NIGHTTIME SAN DIEGO sparkles at the edge of one of the finest natural harbors in the world. Beyond the tall buildings of downtown, the curved finger of San Diego Bay extends for fifteen miles, sheltered by North Island and the long, high bulk of Point Loma.

SAN DIEGO 175

VISIBLE REMINDERS OF A SPANISH PAST still remain in San Diego. The one that most vividly recreates the hospitable atmosphere of those leisurely years is Ramona's Marriage Place (ABOVE), *built in 1825 and used as the setting for Helen Hunt Jackson's famous novel* Ramona. *The plain façade of the San Diego Mission* (RIGHT) *wears an air of simple dignity befitting its position as the first in the chain of the missions.*

A LANDMARK of San Diego's Balboa Park, the richly ornamented California Tower rises high above a beautiful Moorish style garden patterned after the famous Alcazar Gardens of Seville, Spain. The older buildings in the park and many of the magnificent plantings date from the international exposition held on the site in 1915-1916. San Diegans ever since have taken proud delight in the rococo detailing, long shaded arcades, and luxuriant semi-tropical gardens.

178

*TURRETS AND CUPOLAS and hundreds of windows ornament the noble old Hotel del Coronado, a marvel of Victorian architecture dating from the era of resplendent resort hotels. Since the elaborate structure opened in 1888, it has carried forward a tradition of impeccable service in opulent surroundings that conjures visions of visiting royalty and presidents, of varnished hacks rolling under the porte cochère, of grand balls beneath the great crystal chandeliers, and of elegant banquets served in the grand manner in the enormous, high-vaulted Crown Room. Across the road from the hotel grounds, the picturesque little hotel boathouse (*ABOVE*), now a restaurant, hugs the shore of Glorietta Bay.*

180   SAN DIEGO

SAN DIEGO   181

A SPARKLING PLAYGROUND of boating channels, islands, sheltered coves, sandy beaches, and trim marinas, Mission Bay Park's vast area (4,600 acres) is a showplace of bold civic planning. Once a dismal tide-flat, the bay now teems with activity. It can accommodate a sailing regatta, a hydroplane race, and speedboat races — all at the same time, without interfering with water skiers, swimmers, and fishermen in other areas. Around its shore, attractive resorts display unusual, sometimes playful, architecture. And just a few blocks away, the ocean surf rolls against the long expanse of Mission Beach.

ROY KRELL

ROY KRELL

SAN DIEGO   183

PANORAMA AND HISTORY are set forth at Cabrillo National Monument at the tip of Point Loma. Old Point Loma light stands atop the headland's high point. Its lens, one of the first on the coast, came from Paris and was first lit in 1855. Down the hill from the lighthouse, the buildings of the Visitors' Center spread over a knoll above Ballast Point, where Juan Rodrigues Cabrillo, the first European to see this shore, landed in 1542. Beyond the busy bay, with its armada of grim, gray war vessels mingling with frivolous little pleasure craft, the chalky buildings of San Diego ascend the slope of a natural amphitheater and recede into the purple hills.

*TOWERING WAVES explode against the sandstone cliffs of La Jolla in
a spectacular display of awesome power. Wave-cut arches and caves pierce
the cliffs around La Jolla Cove, where scuba divers and tide-pool
explorers look for prizes in the clear water and undersea gardens. Above
the coastal bluffs and beaches stand the homes and apartments of the town,
a famed resort since the 1880's.*

*SERENE AND SILENT, four sailplanes soar like eagles on the rising
air columns off the cliffs of Torrey Pines Mesa. The steady flow of air that
supports the pilots in their free flight also torments the plant materials
that grow along the brow of the cliffs. The forceful winds shape the pines for
which the mesa is named into forms of grotesque beauty, with twisted
branches that seem to be warding off the unrelenting wind.*

188

JOSEF MUENCH

*IN A PLEASANT VALLEY, the red-trimmed San Luis Rey Mission,
completed in 1802, reposes in the afternoon sun. The bronze bells in the
campanario no longer summon hundreds of Luiseno Indians to worship or to
work. In its prime, this was the largest mission in the chain, and its
buildings ranged over six and a half acres. All that now remains of much of
the original cloisters is a procession of plastered adobe arches, vaguely
reminiscent of an ancient Roman aqueduct.*

FROM MOUNT PALOMAR, a sweeping panorama of green valleys and rows of tumbled mountain ranges recedes into the misty horizon. On Palomar's summit, the great silver dome of the observatory looms incongruously above the pines and oaks. Inside, the world's largest telescope photographs stars billions of miles away.

SAN DIEGO 193

THE DESERT

The desert casts a spell over all who know it well. A strange and lonely land, a place of mystery and of violent extremes, of serenity and stillness, it exerts a hypnotic pull that draws men to its haunting beauty.

In its natural state, the desert stretches in seeming emptiness to the far, purple hills in a shimmering vista of great serenity. Around its horizons run the bare, treeless mountains, stripped to the naked earth by abrasive winds and flash floods. The exposed soil reveals itself in bizarre reds, browns, blacks, and yellows that become transformed by the haze of distance into magenta, blues, and purples. The eroded mountains, boldly sculptured by the cutting wind and water, present stark shadow patterns in the slanting rays of morning or late afternoon.

At the base of the richly colored hills spreads a treeless plain of sandy gravel or an ocean of sand dunes, raked by the wind into frozen wave patterns. Low, gray creosote bushes dot the high desert area, interspersed with prickly cactus plants of an enchanting virtuosity of form or the disjointed figures of Joshua trees spaced out over the plain.

In the raw desert, the handiwork of man is seldom apparent. No windbreaks limit the horizon, no farmhouses or windmills catch the eye, no crops cover the land. The feeling of isolation is intensified by the profound stillness that makes even the littlest sound seem important—the faint scrabbling of a lizard or a bird in the dry scrub, the whisper of a warm breeze that comes from nowhere and goes nowhere.

The desert reveals the arrival of spring long before the rest of the state awakens. A carpet of lavender sand verbena colors the sandy washes, orange poppies flame over the hills of the Mojave, and tamarisks open like puffs of pink smoke. The whiplike ocotillos burst out with bright red fringes, yuccas hold their snowy plumes aloft, and the cacti display exquisitely formed, waxy flowers. The show does not last long—for summer also comes early and turns its unrelenting heat upon the plants.

The desert is unforgiving to those who break its rules, but men have learned to tame its harshness and to put the land to practical uses. Thousands of acres of wasteland have been reclaimed by irrigation and the fertile sandy soil made to burgeon forth with bumper crops of cotton, melons, and lettuce. In the towns, vacation colonies, and resorts that are scattered throughout, residents live the year around in air-conditioned comfort, and vacationers flock to the resorts to soak up the warm winter sun.

JOHN ROBINSON

WILLIAM APLIN

UNION PACIFIC RAILROAD

WATER TRANSFORMS THE SANDY WASTES of the desert.
An irrigation canal zigzags across the flat land between neatly engraved acres
of rowcrops and regiments of fruit trees. Elsewhere in the desert, winter
rains bring forth colorful displays. Sand-verbena blooms in the Coachella
Valley (RIGHT), while snow still clings to 11,400-foot Mount San Gorgonio.

196

*A ROAD TO NOWHERE follows
a precarious ridgetop route in the
sunbaked Mud Hills of Anza-Borrego,
a wild, dry wasteland of folded hills,
alkali sinks, and vast stretches of
creosote and cholla, relieved here and
there by the dot of a green oasis or
a fringe of palms running up a
canyon slit in the mountains.*

199

WILLIAM APLIN

THE DESERT BLOSSOMS in rich variety. Tough, wiry plants, uniquely adapted to the thin soil, searing sun, and lack of rain, thrive on the arid wastes. Shaggy, contorted Joshua trees stand silhouetted against rocky hills in the first light of dawn. Spring comes in a pastel wash of evening primrose and sand verbena spread over the dunes, or in the spectacular show of the plumed yuccas, holding their snowy flames high above the desert scrub.

*THE DEADLY BEAUTY of the desert is nowhere more discernible than in the wastes of the Death Valley sink (*ABOVE*), where the icy crests of the Panamints reflect unblemished in the still water of a poisonous, alkaline pool at Badwater, 279 feet below sea level. Farther south, near the Mexican border, a lonely hiker sets out across the magnificent Algodones dunes. Here, in recent years, footprints of hikers have been joined by the tire tracks of modified roadsters called dune buggies.*

DEEPLY ETCHED *by the wind and occasional cloudbursts that sluice down their exposed flanks, the barren mountains of the Death Valley badlands present a shadowy pattern of rich browns and yellows in the early morning sunlight.*

THE DESERT   205

THE SOUTHERN MOUNTAINS

Around the inland edges of the Los Angeles plain looms a vast amphitheater of mountains, composed of a series of ranges bearing musical Spanish names—the Santa Monicas, San Gabriels, San Jacintos, and Santa Anas—and offering from their crests some of the most unusual visual contrasts in California.

The mountains rise abruptly from near sea level and ascend several thousand feet, reaching a climax in four towering peaks that are more than 10,000 feet in height. Dry and barren on their lower slopes, they turn green as the altitude increases and reach a forested crest, set with mile-high lakes.

The traveler winding his way up the grades runs in a few miles through a succession of life zones equivalent to a trip from Mexico to northern Canada. In short order, he passes from palms and cactus through hills mantled with chaparral, thence into forests of ponderosa pine, incense cedar, and fir, and finally emerges in an alpine setting of lichens and mosses, far above timberline. From a wooded crest, he can look down to the silvery desert, simmering in the heat 8,000 feet below.

Easily accessible, the ranges are broached by broad, double-track freeways that climb in bold sweeps through wide, open passes and give access to slow-paced highways that twist their way up the canyons to reach the sparkling lakes and shady, resinous forests of the upper elevations. Many of the drives are notable scenic experiences in themselves: the Rim-of-the-World Drive, Angeles Crest Highway, and Palms-to-Pines Highway disclose frequent vistas of breathtaking scope—views of sharply eroded desert hills of red and purple, of wooded slopes jumbled together in ascending ridges, or of the incredible metropolitan sweep, especially sensational after dark when the twinkling cities light the black plain as far as the eye can see.

The march of the seasons draws the Angeleno to the heights to enjoy the changes that are barely perceptible in the mild climate of the lowlands. In spring, wildflowers and blossoming shrubs brighten the lower slopes with a colorful tide that slowly advances up the mountainsides as the season moves into summer. The rainless months cast a hot, dusty spell over the forests that lasts until the relief of the first fall storms, which rinse the boughs, soak the needle-carpeted soil, and fill the air with a bracing fragrance. Autumn flashes briefly and gives way quickly to winter, signaled by heavy snowfall in the higher elevations. People throng to the winter playgrounds to ski or toboggan; many come to enjoy their very first contact with snow.

HORST AHLBERG

WALTER HOUK

WALTER HOUK

SOUTHERN MOUNTAINS   207

208   SOUTHERN MOUNTAINS

A CHECKERBOARD PLAIN, cut by a wandering, seasonal river, spreads out below Mount Wilson, terminating at the Santa Ana Mountains on the far-off horizon. At night, the panorama of the skies is studied by the telescopes housed beneath the silvery domes of Mount Wilson's observatory.

SOUTHERN MOUNTAINS 209

WITHIN A FEW MILES, the southern mountains offer surprising extremes. Cajon Pass, snaking its way through the San Gabriel Mountains on its way to the desert, runs for miles through dry, gray, sage-covered ranges. Always in sight, the snow-dusted, 10,000-foot hump of Old Baldy towers on the horizon. On the other side of the snowy crest lies a highly developed winter sports area, where skiers can glide among crystalline trees in a setting of silence and tranquility.

SOUTHERN MOUNTAINS   211

A FIFTEEN-MINUTE RIDE takes the visitor by aerial tramway
from the heat of the desert and the sun-drenched resorts of the Palm
Springs area to the 8,500-foot level of the San Jacintos. On the rocky
mountain crest, wind-torn trees cling to the meager soil above barren,
gullied slopes that drop down to the desert in the hazy distance.

SOUTHERN MOUNTAINS   213

MANTLED IN WHITE, Lake Arrowhead Village is transformed into a postcard scene by a heavy winter snowfall. Thick snow clings to the roofs of the chalets, drips off the eaves in glistening icicles, and chokes the streets in massive drifts. Skiers and other snow enthusiasts throng to this winter playground just three hours from balmy Los Angeles. In another season, the lake appears in a different guise. The sun sparkles on a surface usually lively with sail and power boats, and summer visitors fill the cabins and resorts around the pine-covered shore.

THE SIERRA NEVADA

No one who has ever watched the alpenglow on Half Dome fade into forgetfulness, or seen puffy white clouds scudding across Lake Tahoe, driven by winds that roar through the treetops like freight trains crossing a trestle, or who has stood in reverent awe in the presence of the Giant Sequoias can ever forget the majestic world of the Sierra Nevada.

Within the boundaries of this granite domain are countless visual experiences that linger in the memory. Rivers foaming over rocky beds in the full tide of spring, or gently meandering along in the last leisurely trickle of fall. Waterfalls that drop hundreds of feet in a gauzy torrent that shakes the ground with the force of the falling tons of water; or gentler falls that cascade down in a veiled mist that captures the rainbow in its spray. Rocky, conifer-rimmed lakes that sparkle in the morning sun, as the breezes chase each other across the smooth surface, or turn to choppy gray in the afternoon when the wind churns the surface into whitecaps that slam against the boats that drone across the troubled water. Quiet meadows, dressed with blue lupine or yellow monkey flowers, where deer graze and an occasional bear shuffles across, following a favorite path.

Crystal-clear nights that seem to reveal more stars than ever existed before. Brief, violent electrical storms that smash against the granite peaks, echoing and re-echoing in wild counterpoint, and then move on, grumbling, to cannonade some distant range.

The bright splash of autumn, changing the tall trees to pillars of orange, scarlet, and yellow that slowly shed their saucer-size leaves in graceful showers. And finally, the white blanket of winter that seals the high passes, calls out the skier to test the powdery snow, and settles a pure crystalline stillness over the frosted land.

The enumeration could be continued indefinitely without exhausting the memorable features of the Sierra. It is sights and experiences such as these that reward those who come to the Sierra, no matter how briefly, with physical renewal and spiritual refreshment.

The Sierra Nevada (Spanish for "snowy range") has been authoritatively defined as "the longest, highest, and the grandest single mountain range in the United States." Rising gradually in the west to its 7,000 to 14,000-foot crest, the range drops off abruptly to the east into a long desert-like trough. The majestic mountain complex runs nearly 400 miles along the backbone of the state, from Lake Tahoe to Walker Pass.

MARTIN LITTON

MARTIN LITTON

MARTIN LITTON

SIERRA NEVADA 217

EAST OF THE SIERRA,
a storm hovers above the Inyo
Mountains across the Owens
Valley, leaving a light dusting
of early snow. The gnome-like
rocks of the Alabama Hills
in the foreground, some as
large as five-story buildings,
are thought to be the oldest
rock formation on this
continent.

POWELL AND EDNA JENKINS

219

MIKE HAYDEN

THE LURE OF THE TROUT draws fishermen to the eastern Sierra,
where quiet lakes reflect a grand backdrop of tumbled mountain peaks.
In autumn, delicate aspen trees frame the peaks behind Bishop Canyon (RIGHT),
and at Silver Lake (ABOVE), *a lone angler tries for the wily big fellows.*

THE JAGGED, SNOW-COVERED SCARP of the Sierra Nevada is bathed
in radiant light in the early dawn, while the low hills below still slumber in the
shadow, and animals graze quietly on the broad grasslands.

ANSEL ADAMS

SIERRA NEVADA 223

A PEACEFUL LAKE in the Mammoth area lies cupped in a tranquil basin, rimmed by forests of pine and fir and enclosed by the looming wall of the Sierra escarpment. Near timberline, the surrounding mountains are covered with alternating swaths of forest and talus slides of naked granite. Over the hump of the Sierra and down at the foot of a rough, winding road, the Devils Postpile (ABOVE) presents a fascinating spectacle of massed basaltic prisms.

RAY ATKESON

226   SIERRA NEVADA

*BLUE-GREEN PINE FORESTS encircle jewel-like
Emerald Bay, Lake Tahoe's greatest scenic attraction, and
beyond the gap in the forest, the shimmering reaches of
the azure lake stretch to the Nevada mountains. On a wintry
day, the jumbled rocks of Rubicon Point (ABOVE) stand
silhouetted against gathering thunderheads, and the water
stirs restlessly in the presence of the approaching storm.*

SIERRA NEVADA   227

SERPENTINE TRACKS cut through the thick white mantle that covers the Sierra for part of every year. Little-traveled roads remain hidden until the sun finds them in the spring, but through highways are kept open by giant snowplows, giving skiers access to the powdery runs of the Sierra's winter sports centers.

229

230 **OMINOUS STORM CLOUDS,** *swirling above the walls of Yosemite Valley, amplify the dramatic grandeur of this incomparable vista. Great domes and pinnacles stand out against the sky, and sparkling waterfalls tumble from the cliffs.*

ANSEL ADAMS

MAJESTIC HALF DOME rises 4,800 feet above the floor of Yosemite Valley. At its feet, the Merced River, icy cold in early spring and swollen with the snowmelt from the High Country, flows swiftly down the canyon. This is a scene known around the world, yet it remains perpetually fresh to the viewer whether he sees it for the first or the hundredth time. Later in the year, autumn brings its magic to the Valley and splashes of golden color stand out brilliantly against a background of blue-gray granite.

232   SIERRA NEVADA

AWAY FROM THE CROWDS, the Valley is a quiet place, where deer
splash across the river in peace and the oak leaves shimmer delicately in
the breeze against a backdrop of sheer, glistening granite.

IN EARLY MORNING,
the motionless surface of Mirror
Lake duplicates the beauty of
the surrounding mountains with
crystal clarity. Not a ripple
mars the perfection of the
reflected image.

236

ANSEL ADAMS

A SNOW-DUSTED HALF DOME looms above the valley as winter descends on the High Country. The white blanket disappears quickly from the valley floor 3,000 feet below, but the snowpack builds up in the surrounding mountains, and in the full tide of spring, the rivers fill and thunder over the cliffs in unbridled torrents.

239

TUMBLING RIVERS and sparkling streams, massive mountain peaks, and the largest trees in the world are embraced by the boundaries of Sequoia and Kings Canyon National Parks. The Kings River (ABOVE) *follows a rocky course through a beautiful canyon. To the south, the Generals Highway* (RIGHT) *winds through airy groves of tall, sturdy sequoias. These titans of the forest have withstood the onslaughts of fire, lightning, disease, drought, and crushing snows — some of them for more than two thousand years.*

240   SIERRA NEVADA

THE HIGH COUNTRY of the Sierra Nevada is so vast that even an aerial view encompasses a mere sampling. In this panorama, the terrain ranges from Mounts Williamson and Whitney on the left horizon to Kaweah Peaks Ridge on the right, and sweeps down to the Rae Lakes in the left foreground. The John Muir Trail zigzags through this shining land, starting at Mount Whitney, wandering off to the right, then swinging left to leave the picture at Rae Lakes.

242   SIERRA NEVADA

JOHN MUIR TRAIL
winds along the crest of the Sierra in a lofty wilderness uncrossed by any road. Over the years, the passage of thousands of boots and hooves along the trail has worn a furrow in high meadows such as this one below Pinchot Pass.

247

*NO ROADS MAR THE MEADOWS, the white sandy "shores," or
the sparse forests of scattered foxtail pine. From the summit of 11,000-foot
Cottonwood Pass* (LEFT), *one of the gateways to the High Country
from the Owens Lake area, you look across the gentle Kern Plateau to
the snow-spotted spurs of the Great Western Divide beyond the unseen glacial
canyon of the Kern River. Farther to the north* (ABOVE), *the summit of
Mount Whitney* (14,495 feet), *king peak of the Sierra system, reveals a
majestic panorama of glacier-sculptured peaks and chasms.*

249

THE GOLD COUNTRY

For ten tumultuous years, an army of a quarter of a million young fortune-seekers turned a strip of the California foothills upside down in an epidemic quest for gold. The land that they worked over has never been the same since—nor for that matter has the state of California, which was catapulted from a lazy Spanish outpost to a full-fledged state of the Union by the impact of this explosive invasion.

The foothill area that the miners assaulted rolls pleasantly over the lower western slopes of the Sierra Nevada. Part-way between valley and mountain, it is a transitional mixture of chaparral-covered hills, pine forests, and open grassy fields shaded by scattered oaks. High enough to feel the bite of the seasons, the countryside bursts out in riotous color in fall and blossoms forth in spring with bright carpets of wildflowers. In summer, the open hills bake in dry and dusty somnolence.

Into this pastoral wilderness, the Fortyniners burst with pick and goldpan. Almost immediately, they established settlements of varying permanence and repute and labeled them with preposterous names such as Bogus Thunder, Git-up-and-git, Gomorrah, Humbug, Bed Bug, and a hundred others. A rambunctious, hard-drinking and hard-living lot, the men led a toilsome life, most of them on the thin edge of hardship and privation. Robberies, murders, and hangings were not uncommon; and the wooden towns were frequently wiped out by fire. The cannier merchants and residents learned to protect themselves and their valuables by building stone structures with sheet-iron roofs and steel-shuttered doors and windows. Some of these buildings are still in use, but many of them are now eyeless and roofless shells.

The wild growth of the area ended almost as abruptly as it began, but so vigorous and widespread was the impact of the Gold Rush on this compact area that its imprint still shows more than a century later. The scattered relics are tantalizing to view and to explore. The ghostly presence of the miners seems everywhere, haunting the vine-grown ruins, the pathetic graveyards with the teetering headstones, and the windowless churches. The museums and restored towns (most notably Columbia) intensify an illusion that the vanished men have just left for a few days and will soon be back to resume their digging. It is not difficult to imagine them out there in the hot hills, drenched in sweat, pausing in their labors to listen to the insistent, head-drilling buzz of the cicada that fills the sage-scented air.

MASON WEYMOUTH

*EVERY KEYHOLE in every rusty iron door, every boarded-up hole
and gaping doorframe is a window into the lusty past of the Gold Country.
With pathetic grandeur, the staunch masonry walls stand in crumbling
defiance of time, monuments to the optimism of long-forgotten Forty-niners
who built securely in a temporary world.*

MARTIN LITTON

GOLD COUNTRY   253

*BELFRIES AND STEEPLES, some old, some new, rise above
many a quiet scene in the Gold Country. Near Downieville, the soft light
of early morning spotlights a Catholic Church (LEFT) built in 1858, and on
a hillside at the north end of Mariposa, California's oldest courthouse
(ABOVE) is still in service, little changed since it opened in 1854. The
clock in its tower has tolled out the hours since 1866.*

A HUNDRED YEARS AGO, La Porte (ABOVE), *now serene in its tree-rimmed setting, was a bustling, brawling center for hydraulic miners who turned their powerful nozzles on the mountains and washed out gold hidden deep inside. In so doing, they reshaped the landscape and created such strange sights as the Malakoff Diggings* (RIGHT), *where the exposed, multi-colored cliffs rise above milky-blue, man-made lakes.*

256

*WEATHERED
CHURCHES, with their
poignant, weedy graveyards,
seem to be waiting for the
return of the devout miners
who built them, filled their
pews, and sang in their choir
lofts a century ago — and
then suddenly moved on to
fairer lodes, abandoning the
chapels and headstones to
the mischief of sun, wind,
and frost.*

BUILDINGS OF THE PAST are still in use in the Gold Country.
Behind the elegant, wedding-cake façade of old Firehouse No. 1 in
Nevada City, the Nevada County Historical Museum transports visitors
back to Gold Rush days. The town burned twice before this firehouse was
built, but apparently the new firefighters did their job well, for Nevada
City still has many gracious buildings dating from the 1850's.
When the little town of French Corral enjoyed brief prosperity as a center
for placer mining, the simple wooden building above served as its hotel.
In later years it became the town's schoolhouse, and today it serves
again—this time as the community center.

*ON THE HIGH SIERRA TRAIL in Sequoia National Park (LEFT),
two hikers pause to savor the immensity of the granite world spread out
before them, far beyond the road's end. The jumbled cliffs and spires rise above
timberline and the last trees cluster together in the glaciated valley below.
Ahead lies Kaweah Gap, high gateway to the Big Arroyo. On the horizon,
12,000-foot Mount Stewart juts into the sky. Farther south, against a
backdrop of snow-streaked mountains, the cold, crystal clear pools in
the Mosquito Lakes basin (ABOVE) lap quietly at their granite banks and the
patches of snow still remaining from the winter's storms.*

SIERRA NEVADA   245

SPRING IN THE GOLD COUNTRY turns the grasslands lush and green. As the days warm, a tide of wildflowers sweeps over the countryside. The fields become splashed with the delicate golden color of the glorious California poppy and tinged blue with lupine. Animals graze peacefully on oak-studded hillsides and alongside rural lanes, and occasionally a traffic-stalling herd meanders calmly across a roadway.

THE CENTRAL VALLEY

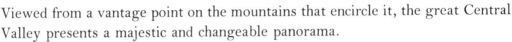

Viewed from a vantage point on the mountains that encircle it, the great Central Valley presents a majestic and changeable panorama.

In the hard light of day, the level miles spread out in a giant's checkerboard, with squares of cultivated land—green orchards and leaf crops, golden wheat, or white cotton—alternating with rich brown acres of fallow soil. Tall windbreaks of cottonwoods and eucalyptus extend the lines of the checkerboard into the air. Lacing through the pattern, the tree-bordered rivers follow wandering courses and the glistening silver ribbons of the irrigation canals trace a zigzag path through the land. Here and there a small cluster of shade trees indicates the site of a ranch house, and a dense grove the location of a crossroad settlement.

At dusk, when the Valley dims with haze and the checkered land recedes from view, the great sink begins to look like an inland sea contained between mountainous shores—as indeed it once was in the geologic past. After nightfall, an inky blackness steals over the land and the empty dark is broken only here and there by the lonely lights of a farmhouse, the twinkling nebulae of a distant city, and automobile headlights moving through the black like lazy fireflies.

Key to the fertility of the Valley's burgeoning acres is the river system, natural and man-made, that awakens the earth with the gift of water. The rivers bring a special way of life into the hot Valley. Nostalgic little towns dream on the wooded banks of the Sacramento, marking the spot where proud sternwheelers once stopped in the heyday of the river. Children swim in the swift currents or fish from leaky skiffs or the bascule bridges. In the crazy-quilt Delta, where the great rivers meet in a jigsaw puzzle of islets and tule-bordered channels, fishing boats poke about in persistent quest of "stripers."

Many of the Valley's cities and towns dating from Gold Rush days have a settled and prosperous air. Their well-kept old homes and shaded streets, canopied by great elms planted by the early settlers, present a picture of peaceful continuity. The spic-and-span relics of historical moment and the massive buildings of the capital in Sacramento testify to the importance of this heartland in the political and social growth of the state.

MARTIN LITTON

STATE DIVISION OF HIGHWAYS

JOSEF MUENCH

A CORDUROY BLANKET of crops spreads as far as the eye can see near Sanger. The immense Central Valley (450 miles long, 30 to 60 miles wide) stands out on topographic maps as a vast, flat surface among California's wrinkles, peaks, and mountains.

THE GRAND SCALE of agricultural operations creates striking patterns.
Sunlight glances off the shimmering surface of a flooded rice field.
In a few weeks, the young plants will break through and hide the water.
Elsewhere, in a setting of pure geometry, rows of leaf crops reach to
the horizon and vanish there in obedience to the classic laws of perspective.

*PARK-LIKE VISTAS here and there interrupt the expanse of crops,
pastures, and orchards. The arching valley oaks of Caswell Memorial Park
(ABOVE) form a shady bower that offers refuge from the searching summer
sun. In spring, a wash of wildflower color sweeps over the great Valley from
bottom to top, and (RIGHT) in Sutter County, acres of golden buttercups spread
out beneath oaks just donning their fresh new leaves.*

270

*THE TWO GREATEST RIVERS in California come together in the
tule-fringed sloughs of the San Joaquin–Sacramento Delta region.
Rising in the snow-melt high in the mountains that enclose the great valley,
the swift-running rivers carry vessels of all sizes and missions.
The towering bulk of a freighter looms among the watchful fishermen like a
whale among minnows, as it noses its way down the deep-water channel,
heading for the open sea. On Georgiana Slough (ABOVE) a sleek sailing vessel
ghosts along on a lazy breeze and hails the crew of an anchored brigantine.*

273

ELEGANT VICTORIAN MANSIONS grace the Valley's towns and cities. John Bidwell, founder of the city of Chico, began work on the handsome house above in 1865. For 62 years, beginning in 1905, California's governors were at home in the Victorian mansion at right. Today both buildings are historical monuments, offering visitors a look backward into history.

274   CENTRAL VALLEY

THE NORTHERN MOUNTAINS

Across the top of the state runs a pocket-sized version of the Sierra Nevada, less well known because of its remoteness but deserving of more attention because of its unspoiled grandeur.

This is a land of isolated lakes, where fishermen can cast into wind-ruffled waters that are rarely disturbed by fishhook and leader; of sun-dappled forest trails and wide meadows speckled with wildflowers, inviting alike to hiker and horseman. This is a backpacker's paradise, where faraway campsites can only be reached by foot or on horseback.

Here is the home of the sentinel peaks, Shasta and Lassen, that rise in solitary majesty above the mountain valleys, the southernmost in a long chain of volcanic mountains that stretches to the tip of the Aleutian Islands. Rectangular Mount Shasta, perpetually capped with snow, turns into a solid cake of glistening white in winter and draws skiers flocking to its chair lifts. Mount Lassen, a slumbering volcano that still emits little wisps of steam and sulfurous smoke, rises aloofly above the scenes of the devastation wrought by its eruption in 1915. In the nearby forests that escaped its wrath, its conical form is mirrored in a ring of crystal lakes, some of them bordered by meadows bedecked with blue larkspur and yellow mule ears. In winter, the peak is mantled with heavy snow, which seals off all access until spring.

Perhaps the best known and certainly most accessible of the Northern Mountains' many spectacles is Shasta Lake, an immense, many-fingered body of water that backs up behind a monumental dam. Its irregular shoreline is spotted with campgrounds and boat-launching sites, and its mountainous shores reverberate to a chorus of outboard motors. Waterskiers and sightseers churn the smooth water; and in the quiet coves, fishermen wait expectantly in their motionless boats.

The mountains are densely forested with Douglas fir and pine, much of it marked for logging. The machinegun staccato of chainsaws sounds through the trees, and the narrow forest roads quake with the passing of giant rigs, carrying logs to the distant mills. Rushing rivers flow down the canyons, foaming over the rocks, and fly-fishermen cast into the current, pitting their wiles against the clever trout.

RAY ATKESON

MARTIN LITTON

MARTIN LITTON

SKY-PIERCING PEAKS *rise from the heartland of the Trinity Alps, and a snow-white mantle drapes over the precipitous slopes. Below the craggy summits, dozens of shining lakes are tucked away in glacial basins.*

*IN THE SNOW-FREE SUMMER, the clear lakes and bosky trails
of the Marble Mountains beckon to those who are willing to leave car
behind. Pack trains wind along cool forest trails into the heart of this
wilderness. The solitary fisherman casts his line into a rock-girt lake that
is a day's hike from the roadhead.*

280

A SHIMMERING SURFACE reflects the radiance of a mountain sunset. The intricate shoreline of Shasta Lake wanders for 365 ragged miles behind mighty Shasta Dam, reaching back into the canyons of the Sacramento, McCloud, and Pit rivers to tap a rugged, forested mountain country laced with rushing streams. Fifty miles to the north, the mountain that supplies the name for both lake and dam rears its sugar-loaf bulk (ABOVE) to 14,162 feet and dominates the landscape for more than one hundred miles.

THE GRAY, GRANITE DOMES and spires of Castle Crags rise
out of an evergreen forest traversed by the Upper Sacramento River. In spring,
the river is a rollicking, white-water stream, with pools and riffles to tempt
the trout fisherman. Farther to the east, Burney Creek bursts out of the side of a
lava wall in McArthur-Burney Falls State Park and drops 132 feet in a
twin stream to the broiling pool below.

NORTHERN MOUNTAINS   285

AWESOME EVIDENCE of the devastation wrought by eruptions of volcanic Lassen Peak spreads over a moon-like wasteland formed by rockslides that raced down nearby Chaos Crags (RIGHT) about 300 years ago. In a more innocent mood, snow-covered Lassen Peak (ABOVE), wearing its cold-weather cap of steam, looks down upon tranquil Manzanita Lake.

Lithographed and bound by Graphic Arts Center,
Portland, Oregon, from lithograph film by
Balzer-Shopes, San Francisco, California.
Type composition by Holmes Typography, Inc.,
San Jose, California.

Front cover: Mission San Antonio de Padua;
photograph by Glenn Christiansen. Back cover:
Carmel Beach; photograph by Steve Crouch.